Money
Smarts

Lucy O'Neill

HIGH
interest
books

Children's Press®
A Division of Scholastic Inc.
New York / Toronto / London / Auckland / Sydney
Mexico City / New Delhi / Hong Kong
Danbury, Connecticut

Special thanks to Founder's Bank, in Media, PA.

Book Design: Michael DeLisio
Contributing Editor: Matt Pitt
Photo Credits: All photos by Maura B. McConnell except p. 11 © Bill
Ross/Corbis; p. 28 Cindy Reiman; p. 32 © Gail Mooney/Corbis; p. 38 Dean
Galiano

Library of Congress Cataloging-in-Publication Data

O'Neill, Lucy.
   Money smarts / by Lucy O'Neill.
   v. cm. -- (Smarts)
   Published simultaneously in Canada.
   Includes bibliographical references and index.
   Contents: Introduction -- Basic banking -- Credit cards and loans --
   Bulls and bears and bonds -- Planning for the future -- New words.
   ISBN 0-516-23929-5 (lib. bdg.) -- ISBN 0-516-24014-5 (pbk.)
   1. Teenagers--Finance, Personal--Juvenile literature. 2. Saving and
   investment--Juvenile literature. 3. Finance, Personal--Juvenile
   literature. [1. Finance, Personal. 2. Saving and investment.] I. Title.
   II. Series.

HG179 .O54 2002
332.024'055--dc21
                              2002002863

Contents

Saving money each week is one of the best habits you can get into — bank on it!

Everything from TV to magazines tells us that spending money will make us happy. Buy this product, or wear these clothes, and your life will be better. Most of us know that money can't really buy happiness. Still, when you have cash in your wallet, it's tough to keep from spending it.

The best way to fight the urge to splurge is to start saving. Saving money for a rainy day may sound boring, but it's a good piece of advice to remember.

Saving is something you can learn at a young age. Say you normally spend your entire weekly allowance on movie tickets. But one day you see a new video game you want to buy. You decide not to see any movies for a while. After a few weeks, you've saved enough money to buy the game. You had to go without something you like. But the reward is that you got something you wanted more.

Every step you take in managing your money builds your self-esteem—and your wallet. When you open your own bank account, it gives you a feeling of independence. You gain confidence by watching your money earn interest and increase in value. You may even be taking steps toward becoming a millionaire!

It's not always easy to pass up on impulse purchases. Yet if you do, you'll end up having more money down the line.

Chapter 1

Basic Banking

Opening a bank account is an easy way to build your financial future. Banks are businesses that keep track of money for their customers.

Check It Out

Checking accounts allow bank customers to write checks to pay for goods and services. Why would you write a check instead of paying with cash? There are several reasons. Let's say that you see a TV commercial for a music CD you want. The announcer gives the address where you should send your payment. But sending cash through the mail can be risky. If it gets lost or stolen on its way, you won't get your CD. Your money will be gone forever.

Having a checking account provides some important safeguards. You can keep your money safely in a bank while purchasing items.

If your check gets lost or stolen, however, you won't lose your money. Your check must reach its destination to be cashed. Once the business receives your check, they take it to a bank. Someone from the business endorses, or signs, the back of the check. The bank matches this signature with one they have on file. This way, they know that the person cashing the check is who they claim to be. Once the bank gives their official approval, the check clears. Your bank then takes the money out of your account, and deposits, or places, it into the business' account. Once a month, your bank mails a statement to you. This piece of paper details all the checks you've written that month. They also send back the endorsed checks.

When you write a check, it's your responsibility to make sure you can cover the amount. If you write a check for ten dollars, and you have two hundred dollars in the bank, it will clear. However, if you have ten dollars in the bank, and try to write a check for two hundred dollars, it will bounce. If you bounce a check, the bank can charge a pretty steep penalty fee.

Most banks guarantee that they will keep all of their customers' money safe and sound.

Some checking accounts require a minimum balance. This is an amount that you must keep in the bank at all times. If your balance drops below this amount, the bank can charge you a fec. When you open an account, it's important to understand all the conditions that the bank requires you to meet.

Some questions you should ask:
- Does the account require a minimum balance?
- Does the checking account give you interest?
- Are there limits to the number of checks that can be written each month? Or is there a per-check fee?
- Is there a monthly account fee?
- Is there a special account geared toward students?

Better safe than sorry: ATM machines come equipped with a small security camera. This camera takes photos of anyone that approaches the machine.

ATM Option

Most banks provide their customers with a system of Automated Teller Machines (ATMs). ATM customers put a card, given to them by the bank, into the machine. The customer can take out money, or put in money, to his or her account. The customer can also find out information about the account. The ATM provides a receipt each time it is used. The receipt tells the customer how much cash remains in his or her account.

The best thing about ATMs is that many can be used 24 hours a day. If you need some emergency cash, ATMs are there for you. Plus, most banks don't charge customers to use their own ATMs.

Heads Up

Fees, Fees, Fees!
Bank fees can be frustrating. Some banks charge penalties if an account drops below the minimum balance. Others charge for using an ATM machine provided by a competing bank or business. Some only allow customers to write a few checks each month before tacking on fees. Most banks charge a monthly service fee of some kind. You should always investigate what charges might affect your account before you open one.

Does It Interest You?

Banks do more than provide a place to store money. Banks also use their customers' money to build savings of their own. They make money off of your money, and pay a little bit back to you. This payment is known as interest.

Interest is paid at a percentage rate called the annual percentage yield (APY). Savings and checking accounts usually pay interest monthly. Other types of accounts may pay interest quarterly, or even annually. However it is paid, the interest is added to your own money. You then earn interest on the total amount. This is called compound interest.

Savings Accounts and CDs

One way to begin earning interest is to open a savings account. A savings account is sometimes called a statement savings, or a passbook savings, account. Most savings accounts allow you to deposit money whenever you want. Most accounts allow you to

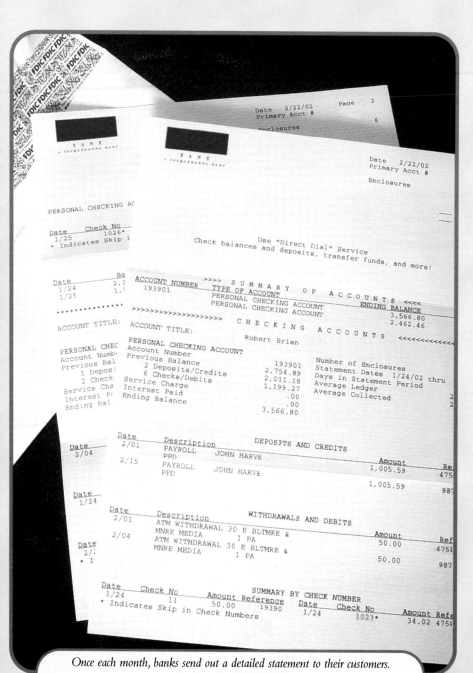

Once each month, banks send out a detailed statement to their customers. This statement lists all account activity from the previous month. Still, it's a good idea to keep up your own personal records.

withdraw, or take money out, without being charged a penalty. Savings accounts provide some interest, but not much. In 2001, average interest rates for savings accounts hit an all-time low of 1.09 percent. That means if you had one hundred dollars in a savings account, you would earn only $1.09 in interest for the entire year.

You may want to explore another saving option: Certificates of Deposit (CDs). To open a CD, you often need to give the bank a larger amount of money than a savings account requires.

CDs earn a greater rate of interest than savings accounts. That's because you agree to leave your money in the bank for a certain amount of time. You agree to keep your money in a CD for three months, six months, or even longer. Penalties apply if you withdraw the money before the end of the agreed term. The longer you leave your money in the CD, the more interest it earns.

Choosing a Bank

It's important to find a bank that works for you. This can be a time-consuming search. That's because there are so many options to choose from. There are large corporate banks, such as Citibank or Chase. Your town probably has smaller, local banks, too. There are even banks that exist only on the Internet!

It may be easiest to open an account at your parents' bank. Since your parents have a history of working with this bank, they can tell you what fees (or rewards!) to expect. Some banks give special offers to new customers.

The Federal Deposit Insurance Corporation (FDIC) insures most banks. The FDIC is a government organization that protects customers. If a bank goes out of business, the FDIC guarantees that bank customers will not lose their money. Their guarantee covers up to $100,000 per bank account.

Be sure to speak with employees from several banks and credit unions. This will make it easier for you to find the best fit.

Credit Unions

Federal credit unions are nonprofit financial institutions. Credit unions are owned and run by the very people who have accounts there. Credit unions are highly democratic. Members elect the leaders that run them. When members borrow money, they know the people who are loaning it. This makes for a tight-knit community.

Sounds like a pretty good club, right? Well, there's a catch. Not everyone can join. Each credit union has a limited membership. For instance, some credit unions only allow teachers to join. Others serve individuals and families who don't make a lot of money. Those that can join credit unions choose them for many different reasons. Some people feel more comfortable working with a local business. Credit unions often provide more personalized attention than chain banks do. Plus, credit unions often choose to charge lower fees than larger banks.

There are some drawbacks, however. Credit unions usually don't have a large network of ATMs. This makes it more difficult to withdraw cash from your account without being charged a fee. Also, the FDIC does not insure credit unions. However, most credit unions have some kind of insurance to protect their customer's money.

Chapter 2

Credit Cards and Loans

Banks and credit unions offer more than just checking and savings accounts. They make it possible for people to borrow money. By borrowing money, people can pay for expensive items, such as cars or college costs.

Loans

A loan is money that a bank gives to a customer for a limited period of time. It is not a gift. You are required to repay the money. You are also responsible for paying interest on the loan. You may need to make payments for several months, or even years.

Many young people going to college take out loans to pay for tuition. When asking the bank for

Pick a card, any card: Credit card companies make a lot of money off of young people. Many of these companies tend to charge the highest interest rates to their youngest customers.

money, you fill out a loan application. The application asks for information about your financial history. You will have to list any collateral you have. Collateral is property you own that the bank can take if you fail to repay the loan. For example, let's say Steve receives a loan for a new car. The car itself might become the loan's collateral. If Steve fails to repay the loan, the bank can legally take his car away. This is known as repossessing the car.

Younger people usually don't own cars or homes, though. Therefore, they can't provide much collateral. If you apply for a loan while you're still a student, the bank will probably ask a parent to co-sign the application. Your parents' property will be used as collateral.

Give Me Some Credit

Though you may not realize it, credit cards are loans. A credit card allows you to purchase items without paying for them immediately. Banks provide many of these credit cards. Even businesses, such as department stores and gas stations, can offer them.

It's very easy to find a shop or store that will accept your credit card. Just remember to pay your debts quickly—don't let them slide.

If your credit card gets lost or stolen, be sure to call the credit card company and report it right away.

You can use a credit card to buy almost anything you want. That is, until you reach the credit limit that your credit card company has given to you. Each month you will be sent a bill for your purchases. You can pay your bill all at once. Or, you may choose to pay the amount little by little, over many months. However, if you choose this option, you're charged interest. Until you pay off your bill, the amount of interest that you owe will increase every month–even if you don't buy anything new! Interest rates on credit card purchases are usually very high. The interest is calculated using the Annual Percentage Rate (APR). The APR is the total amount of interest charged each year.

A credit card can make life more convenient. Instead of carrying a lot of cash, you can use your credit card to make purchases. Virtually every kind of business accepts them. Let's say you want to buy a plane ticket. You don't have enough money saved for it now. However, the job you've just started will help pay it off. You can use your credit card to purchase the plane ticket now. Then you'll pay off the credit card bill once your paychecks start arriving.

As long as you carefully pay off your balance, carrying a credit card should cause no problems. However, credit cards make it easier to be careless with money. It can be tempting to buy things you can't afford because you have that plastic card in your pocket.

DeShawn's Story

"The summer after I graduated high school, I worked at a mall. I took the job to earn money for college. On my first day, a sign in a department store at the mall caught my eye. The store was making a special offer to new customers. They were offering an extra 10 percent off all purchases if I opened a credit card with the store. They processed my application on the spot. Even though I didn't have much money, I was approved in five minutes. I went shopping that first day and spent one hundred dollars. It felt like magic, being able to shop without taking cash out of my wallet. I didn't think about how long I would have to work to earn the money to pay my bill.

A month later, my first bill came. I had already used the card a few other times. My balance was one hundred-fifty dollars. It was a lot of money, but I wrote a check for twenty-five dollars. I figured I'd pay the rest off by the end of the summer. I continued using the card for little things. Before I could blink, my second bill came. I was shocked to see that I was being charged 19 percent interest! If I was even one day late with my payment I was charged an additional twenty-dollar late fee.

My mother told me to cut up the card. I felt stupid doing that. Still, I'm glad I took her advice. It took a lot of work for me to finish paying off the

Owning a credit card can make you feel like you have access to free money. Yet for some young people, cutting their cards is the best way to free themselves from debt.

Credit card companies like to hook people in by using big promotions. If you get a card with a high interest rate, though, that little piece of plactic could seem like an 800-pound gorilla.

balance. I started college in the fall with less money than I'd hoped, but at least I was debt–free!"

It's easy to get sucked into feeling that having a credit card is the key to an adult life. Don't believe the hype. Credit cards have led many adults into severe debt, owing thousands of dollars to other people or businesses.

Debt Problems

Each year, millions of people must deal with serious debt. If you're struggling with credit card debt, you can seek help. A credit-counseling agency can sometimes get credit card companies to stop charging interest until your balance is paid off. You must agree to stop using all of your credit cards. The counseling agency helps you create a budget. Based on that bud-

Heads Up

Read the Fine Print

Getting a credit card can be exciting, but read all offers carefully before filling out an application. Credit card companies are in business to make money. They spend a lot of money in advertising to encourage you to join. Department store credit cards can be easy to get. However, they often charge the highest annual interest rates. Other cards offer "no annual fee" or "interest-free for six months" promotions. That's great—but how high is the interest after that? If it sounds too good to be true, it probably is.

get, you make one monthly payment to the agency. The agency then distributes your payments to the individual credit card companies. Gradually, you become debt-free, and the credit card companies receive the money they are owed.

Companies would rather get their money from a credit-counseling agency than see their customers file for bankruptcy. Being bankrupt means that someone cannot afford to pay back the money he or she owes. Bankruptcy legally releases someone in serious financial trouble from all outstanding debts. The companies that lent the individual money are forced to take a financial loss. The companies cannot continue trying to get paid back. Sounds good—but bankruptcy has serious consequences. Filing for bankruptcy is recorded on your credit history. It stays there for ten years. It affects how people consider you for many things, from buying cars to job hunting. Bankruptcy should not be taken lightly—it's a last resort.

Budgets

Though it's not exciting, writing a budget may be one of the best skills you ever learn. First, make a list of your income for one month. Include any jobs, allowance, or other money you have coming in. If your income is wildly different from month to month, take an average of three months. Then make a list of your expenses. List everything you spend

Most dream purchases require a lot of hours of hard work before you can afford the item.

money on during one month: food, clothing, movies, CDs, anything. Subtract your total expenses from your total income. Hopefully, you will have some money left over. It's a great idea to save and invest this amount each month.

If your expense total is the larger number, then you're spending more money than you earn. You should consider ways of cutting costs wherever possible. Coupons and store sales are good ways to cut down your expenses.

Chapter 3

Bulls and Bears and Bonds, Oh My!

Many young people consider investing in the stock market. When you buy stock in a company, you become a part owner of that company. The more of the company's stock you buy, the more of the company you own. Stocks increase or decrease in value each day, depending on how successfully the business performs. When a company performs well, the company's stockholders are paid a share of the profits. These are called dividends.

In the stock market, there are thousands of stocks you can invest in. During some periods of time, most stocks increase in value. This is called a bull market. However, there are also times when

The floors of the stock exchange are filled with people who want to make a quick buck. While some succeed, others lose their money in the blink of an eye.

most stocks are decreasing in value. This is called a bear market. Investors can earn a lot of money by paying close attention to the changing directions of the stock market.

Risky Business

Investing in stocks is much riskier than depositing your money in the bank. Thanks to the FDIC, if your bank goes out of business, you'll still get your money back. If you buy stock in a company that fails, you could lose your money altogether.

So why invest in stocks at all? It's true that investing in stocks is risky. However, successful stocks can make a lot of money in a short time. If you put your money in a savings account at 2 percent interest, you won't earn much in a year. But if you invest in stocks that perform well, your money might increase by 5 percent, 10 percent, or even much more. The sky's the limit, and it may only take months! But there are no guarantees, and you can lose money just as quickly. It's best to start investing in the stock market slowly.

Who Can Help?

Before investing in stock, invest some time into talking with relatives who own stock. You can also seek a financial advisor's help, but this costs money. Some advisors get paid on commission. This means their fee is determined by the success of your investments. Other advisors, or brokers, work for a flat fee—others at an hourly rate.

Bonding With Tomorrow

Want to try a popular and safe way to save? Purchase a United States Savings Bond. When you buy a Series EE bond, you pay only half the bond's value. In other words, you can buy a one hundred dollar Series EE bond for just fifty dollars. Each year, your bond will gain interest. Eventually, it will be worth one hundred dollars. The downside to bonds is that they increase in value slowly. It may take ten or even fifteen years to reach full value of the bond. On the other hand, if you need to cash a Series EE bond before it reaches its full value, you won't be penalized.

Chapter 4

Planning for the Future

Buying a house? Investing in the stock market? While you're still in school, such things can be hard to imagine. What if you started your first job last week? It's probably hard to see yourself retiring. However, if you start saving now, you'll create a secure future for yourself ahead of time. You will be prepared if a health emergency or other dangerous event threatens you.

Cassandra's Plan

Cassandra was determined to become a millionaire. With her parents' help, she came up with a plan. She started to put her plan into action by working part-time through high school. By the time she was

Writing down the smallest details of your budget is an important part of realizing your biggest dreams.

Thanks to the help of financial institutions like this one, Cassandra was able to build on her dreams.

eighteen, Cassandra had $2,000 in her savings account. With the help of a local financial planner, Cassandra was able to find an investment plan. The plan would gain an average annual yield of 10 percent. She took the $2,000 and invested it with the plan.

At the end of the first year, Cassandra's money totaled $2,200. During her freshman year at college she worked at a shoe store. She was able to save another $2,000 from the money she earned there. She added that to her investments, for a total of $4,200. At the end of the second year, still earning 10 percent, Cassandra's balance reached $4,620. Cassandra managed to add $2,000 each year until she was twenty-eight. Each year, her investments earned 10 percent. So by the end of the tenth year, Cassandra's balance was $35,062! She had only invested $20,000 of her own money.

From then on, Cassandra left her balance alone. She kept it invested in the plan. Her money grew a lot during some years, and less during others. It depended on whether her stocks were in a bull or bear market. But their value grew, on average, by 10 percent. So, when she turned thirty, the account was worth $46,668. When she turned forty, the account was worth $121,045. Cassandra wasn't adding to the account. It continued to accrue interest. With each year the account grew larger. At age sixty-three, just past the age of retirement, Cassandra received some wonderful news. Her original $20,000 investment was worth $1,083,871. Cassandra had become a millionaire!

Start Your Future Now

There's no guarantee you'll mirror Cassandra's success. An original investment of $2,000 is a lot of money. However, you can start with a hundred dollars, or even ten dollars. The amount isn't important. What's important is to begin saving now. If you get in the habit, there will always be a financial cushion when you need it.

Retirement is not the only reason to save money. Life is full of unexpected things—from health emergencies to sudden travel. Life-changing events may require extra money. If you've been saving for years, you'll have that extra money. If you don't have the money saved, you'll have to rely on loans or credit cards. This kind of reliance can make it hard to stay independent.

Think of saving money as a step toward your successful future. Use the opportunity to learn about different ways of investing. Your money's value will increase every single month. Before you know it, you may find yourself set for life!

Stop by a bank today—you'll be sealing the deal on a brighter tomorrow!

New Words

accrue to increase in value over the course of a specific time period

Annual Percentage Rate (APR) the interest a credit card company charges per year

Annual Percentage Yield (APY) the amount of interest a person's money can earn in a year

Automatic Teller Machine (ATM) a machine which dispenses cash and accepts customers' deposits

bankruptcy a legal action taken by someone who cannot pay off his or her debts

collateral valuable property a person owns

New Words

credit limit the maximum amount of money a person can spend on a credit card

debt money owed to an individual or business

dividends money a profitable company pays back to its stockholders

interest money earned or owed above its original value

invest using money in ways that will earn interest over time

penalties fees charged by a bank for violating an agreement

repossess taking collateral property from a customer who failed to repay a loan

For Further Reading

Bijlefeld, Marjolijn, and Sharon K. Zoumbaris. *Teen Guide to Personal Financial Management.* Westport, CT: Greenwood Press, 2000.

Green, Meg. *Everything You Need to Know About Credit Cards and Fiscal Responsibility.* New York: Rosen Publishing Group, 2001.

Honig, Debbie. *Growing Money: A Complete Investing Guide for Kids.* New York: Penguin Putnam Books for Young Readers, 2001.

Otfinowski, Steve. *The Kid's Guide to Money: Earning It, Saving It, Spending It, Growing It, Sharing It.* New York: Scholastic, 1996.

Resources

Web Sites

The Motley Fool

www.fool.com/teens

A great site to help teenagers with all kinds of financial planning.

Good Money

www.goodmoney.com

Financial advice for people who want to invest safely, economically, and socially.

Credit Infocenter

www.creditinfocenter.com

A resource that provides information on many different financial subjects.

Credit Union National Association

www.cuna.org

Provides ways to find a local credit union.

Credit Counseling Organizations

Credit Counseling Centers of America
(800) 493-2222

www.cccamerica.com

Debt Counselors of America
(800) 680-3328

www.dca.org

National Foundation for Credit Counseling
(800) 388-2227

www.nfcc.org

Index

Index

About the Author
Lucy O'Neill writes about many topics for young adults. She enjoys spending her spare moments with her twin daughters, Alyssa and Eugenia.